Love Kills Slowly: A collection of Poems

Jolene Sitzman

BookLeaf Publishing

Love Kills Slowly: A collection of Poems

Presentation by *BookLeaf Publishing*

Web: www.bookleafpub.com

E-mail: info@bookleafpub.com

ISBN: 9789357442596

First edition 2023

For Samantha, may you always reach for your dreams and realize it's never too late to follow them. Always be your silly self no matter what the world may tell you to be or do. And know I will always love you, unconditionally.

ACKNOWLEDGEMENT

Thank you to my amazingly talented husband Chris for his love and support and for creating my fabulous cover.

Thank you to Sarah for looking over my shoulder and my work from day one. For always having a keen eye and sound advice (even if I don't always listen).

Thank you both for your unconditional love and support.

"The Tree of Love" was written by my dad before his passing. Thank you Dad for being so loving in all you did.

PREFACE

For the loves of my life...

For each of you showed me how love kills slowly, but what dies is never the same.

First Time

sweetly shy
words come out wrong
don't know what to say
don't know how to act
falling slowly

a quick glance
a knowing stare
a brief smile
knowing lips

slowly sinking
fading fast
hands held tight
skin to skin
let it begin

heart flutters fast
feeling dizzy
feeling light
feeling free

eyes opened wide
locked with you
feels so good
no pain, no hurt
soft and slowly
don't know where I am going

lead me there
take perfect care
falling slowly
fading fast
there's no coming back

Waiting for Nothing

My heart aches and breaks
I sit alone and wait
Tears roll down my cheeks
and fall over my lips
I taste the salt, but do nothing
I sit alone and wait

My thoughts are jumbled with words of
meaningless emotion
they run over and over
in my head never ceasing.
I sit alone and wait

The love I feel is so unreal
I cherish every thought of him
I sit alone and wait
His hands slide around my waist
His arms hold me in a sweet embrace
His kiss lingers on my lips
I sit alone and wait

I am his for all eternity
I've given heart, I've given soul
I can not ask for any more
I sit alone and wait
Together we share all we have
we fight every resistance
Together we'll be forever, yet
I sit alone and wait

Entanglement

Touch of satin around my wrist
tied tight, i enjoy the feel of it.
Silkiness across my eyes
the feeling of being blind.

Heart is racing, pounding
hope they can't hear it yet.
silky sheets, spread beneath
gripped tight the only thing
making this real

Lips linger
fingertips trace
my pulse race.
my body gives me away

Glistening and wiggling
inside and out
wanting to begin
and never wanting it to end

The Game

Her a girl younger than him beautiful
talented
Him a man older than her strong,
experienced

You'd see them together everywhere
They were the perfect pair
She fell in love
and her love was true

He fell in love
and all he said was a lie
She was scared and naive
He was powerful and bold

The pressure built
the wall collapsed
She had lost her innocence
He had won the game.

Blue

Blue is a color that I love.
Bright blues shining in the Heavens above.
Deep dark blues of the oceans below.
Blue in the tight denim that you wear.
Blue in the eyes from which you stare.

Blue is a color that I love.
Blue of the feathers of the bird.
Blue of the cerulean sea.
Blue in the button-up shirt that
hugs your arms.
Blue of the truck you drive.

Blue is a color that I love.
Blue looks so good on you.
I'll always be blue for you.

Prick

Sudden stab
Sharp pain, gasping breath

Let me go
Run away
I feel the chase
Running faster, but it always finds me

Sudden Stab
Sharp pain, please go away

It doesn't make sense
It's not mine what you seek
Let me go

Jealousy pricks

Light as a Feather

To feel when I feel nothing at all
To plan an escape from nothing
Nowhere to go, nowhere to fall
Looking around for something,
anything at all

Set aside the worry, set aside the fears
Place it on the table next to my beer
Keep it neat and tidy don't make an
impact
Check your surroundings
Never look back

Moving forward one step at a time
I'm going to make that climb
Then I'll take that leap
And fall one last time
Falling light as a feather

Paint Pouring Love

Love flows like
the paint on this canvas flows.
Love does not follow a certain path
nor does the paint.

Love goes where it is needed
just as the paint flows into the crevices.
Love flows and fills us up
just as the paint fills the canvas.

Love can be messy at times
just as paint can be messy.
We must remember to see the love
through the mess
just as we see the beauty of the paint
through the mess.

The paints mix and change unexpectedly
across the canvas.
Some colors show through brighter and
bigger, others subdued and small,
woven into the background.
Both become an integral part of the
painting
just as love also mixes and changes
unexpectedly across our lives.

Sometimes love will be big and bright
as it is today
and other days it will be a gentle gesture in
the background of your day.
Both are an integral part of love.

Big and bright
Subdued and small
Messy and unexpected
Filling in cracks and paving paths
Like the paint flows,
may your love flow.

Unravel

You unraveled my world
brought me out of my shell
when I was in hell.

I was simple and naïve,
maybe a little slow.
Looking back
I was right on track.

But I followed your thread,
we wove them together.
For a little while, we were even better.

Silently and quickly we began to change.
Nothing remained the same
I left and you never came.

You unraveled my world.
But I unraveled yours
by simply walking out the door.

Hand in Hand

Love is a walk.
Starts with one toe in front of the other
a gesture of complete faith
that your feet will not fail you.

Love starts out slow.
One foot in front of the other
a simple gesture of holding hands
complete faith that
your heart will not break.

Continuing one foot in front of the other
that walk can grow to a jog.
The chance to take bigger steps
and a chance to fall.

Love continues to grow.
Temptation to pick up the pace
A quick jog, run fast, but remember
love is a walk, not a run.

Take it slow, one step
in front of the next
Trust in love,
Have faith in love

Know when to pick up the pace
and when to slow down.
Love is a walk, not a run.

Blood Ties

Blood drips
Blood pours
Blood is thick
Blood is strong

Tears drop
Tears pour
Tears drown
Tears are thin
Tears are weak

Tears over blood drip and drop
Tears drown while blood pours down
Tears are weak
Blood is strong

Is blood thicker than water?

The Tree of Love

DJ+ML

Every tree has its own shape, strength, durability, size, and beauty; and even flaws which make it unique. Like a tree, our love has grown since we met many years ago.
Loving each other's little flaws making each other come to realize how much we offer one another to the point of making us complete.

Limbs may crack and split, mother nature may cause some damage, but the tree still grows in a majestic way. Until one day the tree will be harvested for lumber- to build a home, make furniture, or perhaps a wood carving to pass on the love.

Even our love may have faltered from time to time. Our love overcame obstacles and grew stronger. Our limbs may break or crack, our beauty may not be on the outside as time goes on, but our love is deep within our hearts and one day like in a movie, we can only hope to pass away in the night. I will love you always until our time is done.

Sunshine

Don't hide away
say you'll stay.
Don't close your eyes
say your lies.

Don't feel for me
say you're my key.
Don't look around
your good-byes I have found.

Don't be mad.
Tell me you're glad.
Don't look back
tell me what I lack.
Don't weep
let me go to sleep.

That Feeling

The way I felt is the way I feel.
I wish it was mutual, but it's not.
I loved his voice.
I loved his smile.
I loved his touch.
I loved his kiss.

I can't understand why I did what I did.
I've said I was scared.
I've said I was looking for something.
I've said it's God's way.
I've said I was thinking of him
and all I've said is true.

The day he knew was the day I died.
He can't understand, he can go on.
He can't trust, he can lie.
He can't wait, he can cheat.
He can't love, he can kill.

As for me I can live again.
I've changed my soul.
I've changed my ways.
My heart will always hold a place for him.
The way I felt is the way I feel.

For You

I would create beautiful works of art
if I thought you would stare at it.

I would write you a novel
if I thought you would read it.

I would sing you the most lyrical
masterpiece
if I thought you would hear it.

I would hold you tight in my arms
if I thought you would feel me.

I would kiss your sweet mouth
if I thought you would taste me.

I'd stand naked before you
if you would only see me.

My life is void
without you in it.

Heavy Weight

Pressing in, holding me down
I can't get up.

The lights are bright and breaking
I can't see.

Forced back down
I can't get up.

Tears fall down my face
I can't stop them.

Air struggles to come
I can't breathe.

The weight is heavy
I can't get up.

Universe

Universe is calling
  ring, ring, ring.
Signs are all around
  if you just slow down.

Be still
  and just feel.
The wind speaks its need
  sweeping away the greed.
Soil seeping between your toes
  absorbing all of our woes.

Rain falling across your face
shattering your will,
daring you to keep pace.
Be still and just feel.
When you slow down
  the signs are all around.

Ring, ring, ring.
  She's calling.
    Answer her.

Endings

Warm embraces
smiling faces
tears falling down
as joy mixes with woe

memories flooding
flashing back and forth
was this yesterday
or from years ago

I see everything clearly
no glasses sit on my face
yet everything is so blurry

Feeling the sun
watching the clouds
bringing the simple joys
Not like today's toys

Confused and lost
Am I coming or going?
When will I be with you?

How long do I have to wait?
Is this the beginning
or the end?

www.ingramcontent.com/pod-product-compliance
Lightning Source LLC
Chambersburg PA
CBHW051752130826
49812CB00033B/1114
* 9 7 8 9 3 5 7 4 4 2 5 9 6 *